IMAGES OF ENGLAND

DUDLEY

DUDLEY GUEST HOSPITAL.

MOAT BRIDGE
AND NORTHERN GATEWAY,
DUDLEY CASTLE

Dudley Castle was besieged by King Stephen
in 1138 and by Cromwell's forces in 1644.

IMAGES OF ENGLAND

DUDLEY

DAVID CLARE

TEMPUS

Frontispiece:
Above: The Guest Hospital originally erected for the first Earl of Dudley as an asylum for workers who were blinded in his limestone works, seen here around 1900.

Below: The clothing style of the gentleman in the bowler hat posing for the photographer dates this picture to just after 1900.

First published 2005

Tempus Publishing Limited
The Mill, Brimscombe Port,
Stroud, Gloucestershire, GL5 2QG
www.tempus-publishing.com

British Library Cataloguing in Publication Data.
A catalogue record for this book is available from the British Library.

ISBN 0 7524 3534 5

Typesetting and origination by Tempus Publishing Limited.
Printed in Great Britain.

Contents

Acknowledgements

I am grateful to all those who have helped me compile this collection. In particular to Ned Williams for his support and patience and for letting me raid his enormous collection of material, to Andy Simpson for his transport pictures, and to Alec Brew for his help and encouragement. It would not have been possible to complete the book without the help of the staff in Dudley Archives, who were also kind enough to let me use pictures from their collection. I am also indebted to my Dudley ancestors, without whom I would not be here today.

Introduction

The oldest inhabitants of Dudley lived in a warm sea. Their occupation of the area lasted millions of years and the evidence is in the fossil remains in the very rocks the town is built on. There is a trilobite on the town's coat of arms. Dudley itself is an ancient town. There is no trace of Roman occupation here, so lacking any other evidence we can assume that the town was probably established in the west midland forest by the Anglo-Saxons in the centuries after the first Germanic settlers arrived, before the Norman Conquest in 1066. The town existed before the Domesday survey of 1086, and St Edmund's church is dedicated to an Anglo-Saxon king. It seems to have taken its name from an early settler called Dud, Dod or Dudda. There is no evidence for this apart from the name of the town itself. Soon after 1066 the Normans built a fortification, the castle, on the limestone hill by the village to subdue the local people. It was one of the few castles mentioned in the Domesday book. It was a wooden building on a mound, replaced later by stone buildings.

French-speaking Norman barons lived in the castle, and over the centuries they became anglicised. The fortunes of the aristocracy in the Middle Ages were largely governed by the fate of the monarch they supported. By the sixteenth century the Lords of Dudley were among the most influential men at court. Queen Elizabeth I visited Edward, Lord Dudley at the castle in 1575. In the English Civil War the family supported the Royalists, unfortunately for them the losing side, and after the castle was besieged in 1644 it was deliberately destroyed as a fortress by the Parliamentarians, although the residential quarters remained. Humble Ward succeeded to the title of Lord of Dudley, and to the castle, by marriage and the Ward family lived there until 1750, when there was a disastrous fire that gutted the living quarters. There would not have been enough water up on the hill to put the fire out. According to local legend, molten lead ran down Castle Hill from the castle roof, possibly encouraging the fledgling local scrap industry. After the family moved out of the burned-out castle it was left to become a romantic ruin, a thing very much in fashion in the eighteenth and nineteenth centuries. The castle was used from the mid-nineteenth century, with Lord Dudley's permission, as a public park for town entertainments such as the annual Dudley Fetes, and it became the home of the zoo in 1937, one of Dudley's foremost tourist attractions.

Dudley claims the title of 'Capital of the Black Country'. As it happens I am one of those who include Wolverhampton in the Black Country for reasons of industrial history and development, but although Wolverhampton town centre is grander and more impressive, Dudley is more typical of the Black Country district, historically a region of small-scale manufacturing and small-scale settlements.

Dudley does not have as much fine and varied architecture as other castled towns in the Midlands, such as Ludlow and Warwick. It would have been a town of half-timbered buildings in the Middle Ages. Some fine Georgian houses and streets were built, but rapid expansion and industrialisation over recent centuries has meant that the town has constantly been rebuilt to suit different needs. The growing population in the nineteenth century needed cheap housing, and lots of it. Better-off inhabitants moved further and further out of the busy centre, from the dirty industrial areas into the surrounding countryside. We have glimpses from old photographs and engravings of the pleasant little country town that Dudley must once have been. There is no point in lamenting this loss; these changes happened all over the region and were a natural part of the development of the towns. What we can regret is that so much of the old town survived until after the Second World War only to fall victim to redevelopment. There were many areas of Dudley that benefited from the wholesale demolition and rebuilding that took place in order to create better homes, schools and roads, but the historic core of the town centre should have been better preserved and protected from commercial developers. There are still some attractive little streets around Market Place and High Street, which were at the heart of the medieval town, but the central market area itself that used to be the pride of Dudley has been changed beyond redemption. On the positive side much is being done to preserve and restore what is left. The borough council has done a detailed study of the conservation needs of the town centre and has plans to bring a much larger portion of Dudley inside a conservation area, incorporating the whole of the medieval town centre from the castle through Market Place and up High Street to the church. Buildings in Wolverhampton Street and Priory Street have been carefully restored to their earlier appearance. Apartments are being created in old buildings, bringing much-needed residents back to the town centre. The borough council is to be commended for its work on listing buildings, creating these conservation areas and seeking to improve the character and appearance of the town.

Other books about Dudley have dwelt on its history, mainly concerning the priory, the castle, the Lords of Dudley, the industrial history and monuments that abound in the area, and on the stories of the working people. Dudley does not have many famous sons and daughters. Most people do not know that Abraham Darby the ironfounder was born here in 1677. Duncan Edwards, the footballer who tragically died young in the Munich air disaster of 1958, is remembered and older readers will know the name of Dorothy Round, the tennis player who was Wimbledon champion twice in the 1930s. Film director James Whale was born in Kates Hill in 1889; he made *Frankenstein* (1931), *Showboat* (1936) and *The Man in the Iron Mask* (1939). Otherwise, Sue Lawley, Lenny Henry, the much-missed Billy Dainty and old-time comedian Billy Russell are the only local celebrities whose names are likely to be widely known outside the region.

For this book I have tried to include pictures and illustrations of those elements of Dudley that make an impression on most people when they visit or think of the town; the castle, the zoo, the Black Country Living Museum, cinemas and theatres, the marketplace and town centre streets and shops, trains and buses. I have also stretched the boundary to include a day trip at the end of the book to the Crooked House pub, just off the Himley Road, as it was a major attraction in the area for locals and visitors in the 1900s. I have not included material on the extensive suburbs and towns that make up the Metropolitan Borough of Dudley today, as they deserve a book of their own to do them justice.

The town itself was badly hit economically by the opening of the nearby Merry Hill shopping centre, which took away some of its trade. The Merry Hill centre is very popular, but has no regional identity or tradition. Similar centres can be found all over the country. The future success of the central shopping area of Dudley lies in building on its particular character, on what makes it special to the people who live there. What I hope will emerge from this book is the message that Dudley was and still is a town on a human scale – a friendly, comfortable place to live, work and shop.

one

About
Dudley

DUDLEY

Dudley's coat of arms had been in use since 1866. On the shield is Dudley Castle keep above an anchor and a Davy lamp (representing industry), a fossilised trilobite and a salamander in flames (the traditional symbol of blacksmiths, representing the furnaces). A new coat of arms was designed in 1957 and the current one in 1975.

The sights Dudley was proud of in the 1920s seem odd today. The opera house, Crooked House pub and Priory Hall still seem interesting, but the hospital, town hall and library would suggest that Dudley had little to offer the tourist or day tripper.

Wren's Nest Hill is a continuation of the outcrop of limestone that also forms Castle Hill. Great caverns were hollowed out of the rock to extract the valuable limestone, one use of which was to purify iron ore. This view, from 1910 or earlier, is familiar today as the area is now a nature reserve.

This drawing illustrates the pillars of rock left by the miners to support the roof of the limestone caverns. The caverns were closed for safety reasons but there is now canal boat access to some of them through the Dudley Tunnel.

Canal Tunnel, Dudley Castle Grounds.

Canal boats moved the raw materials of iron-making – iron ore, limestone and coal – around the Black Country. The Dudley Tunnel, here seen in around 1900, bored straight under Castle Hill through a series of caverns, which are open to visitors today. Boat trips run from the canal wharf and passengers can try their hand at 'legging' the narrowboat through the tunnel, which is what the old boatmen had to do, as there was no towpath for the horses.

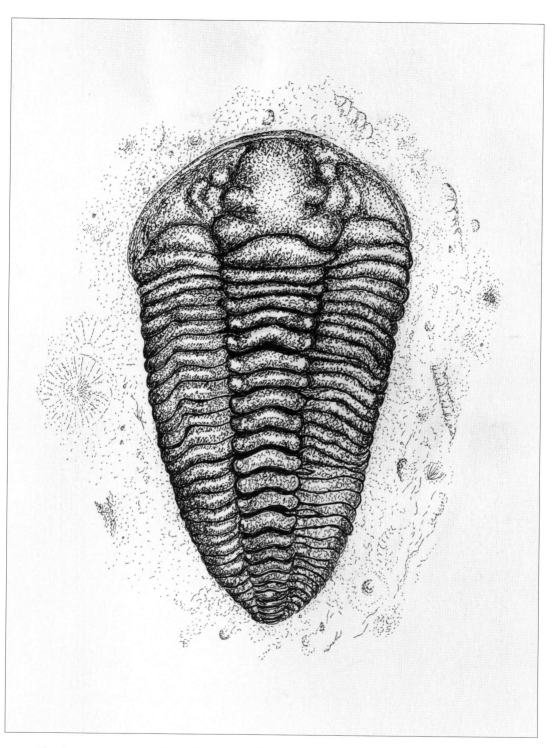

This drawing shows a fossilised trilobite, over 400 million years old, much like the ones found on Wren's Nest Hill. This is probably the type of fossil most familiar to local people; it was so common that it was nicknamed the 'Dudley Locust'.

The blast furnaces of the Black Country consumed enormous amounts of raw materials as steel was produced to satisfy the demand from Britain's booming industries in the nineteenth century. The steel industry was labour-intensive, and judging by the horse-drawn cart not mechanised in 1918, when this card was posted.

In the St James's Road area in the late nineteenth century, the shopkeepers fared little better than their neighbours. There was not much of a living to be made selling goods to the poor.

In times of hardship, Black Country families used to dig up what coal they could find from the pit banks. This scene is at Dudley during the 1926 General Strike, when all coal deliveries ceased for everyone.

The Earl of Dudley owned most of the rights to underground minerals in the area, and the materials were mined with little regard for the buildings on the surface. Houses frequently tilted and collapsed, and streets would suffer from subsidence or the appearance of gaping holes which required urgent repair. The residents could do little but move elsewhere.

Areas of cheap housing for low-paid workers soon deteriorated into slums. These buildings are on St James's Road. The overcrowded courts (seen here in the late nineteenth century) had outside toilets, often shared, and no gardens.

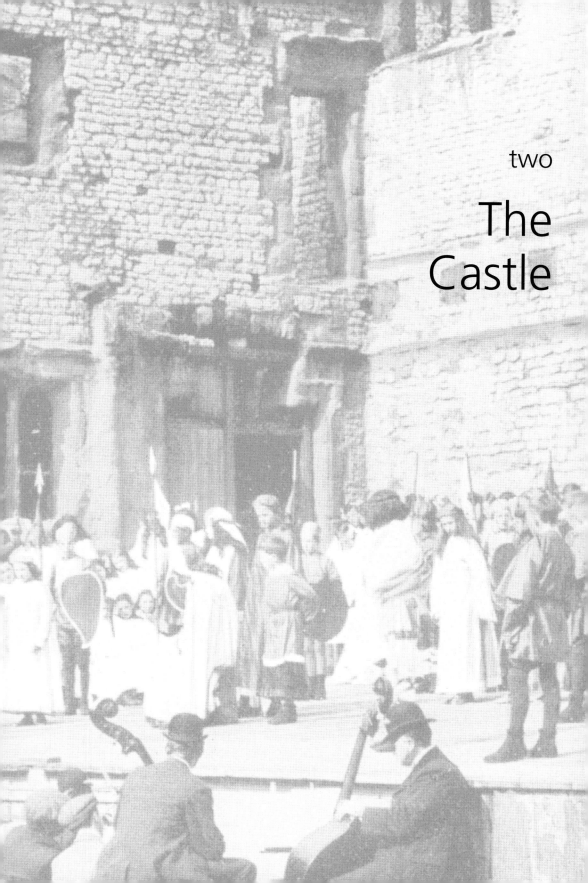

two

The
Castle

Only the earthworks remain of the first castle. The stone walls of the keep, seen in this view of 1912, average 10ft in thickness. The two towers on this side are almost complete, but originally there were two more on the other side; these were destroyed in 1647, during the English Civil War, by the Parliamentarians (the Roundheads).

Children still love to climb on the cannons in front of the castle keep, but a closer look reveals that these are adults posing for the camera in about 1900. The cannons are not original – they were captured during the Crimean War in the 1850s and brought here.

This card was posted in 1907. The castle keep was built in stone in the fourteenth century on the site of the first Norman keep, which would have been made of wood. The Norman castle is one of the few mentioned in the Domesday book, which was compiled in 1086.

This is the extensive range of buildings which remained after the disastrous fire of 1750. From the left, we can see the gateway, the servants' block, the larder and pantry, the kitchen (with the two gables), the buttery (with the bow window) and the Great Hall. This postcard dates from around 1900.

This postcard (from the 1920s or '30s) shows the well-preserved frontage of the sixteenth-century kitchen wing. The soft stone detailing has weathered badly since, however, and there have been no upper floors or roof since 1750.

The watchtower, with its extensive view over the countryside (seen here in about 1900), reminds us that the castle was built as a fortified stronghold by the Normans to maintain control over the English population. When it was newly-built, the castle must have been an awe-inspiring sight perched up on the rocky heights over the small English settlement. There would have been much less tree cover to spoil the view then.

The courtyard of the castle is seen here from the highest point of the keep in the early years of the twentieth century. Castle keeps were heavily fortified and often sited on high ground or man-made mounds, so as to provide a clear view of an attacking enemy.

This view of the courtyard in about 1900 was used on a Christmas postcard. Like many pre–First World War cards it was tinted in approximate colours by the printer, and the main supplies came from Germany, famous for its fine printing. All of this stopped on the outbreak of war in 1914, when trade with Germany became impossible.

The Dudley Castle Fetes Committee of 1867 poses with the band of the First Life Guards. The stovepipe hats were typical of the period, as were the relaxed poses of the men. When you had to hold a pose for a considerable amount of time, it was usually advisable to sit or lie down.

The native chorus goes through a rehearsal for the Dudley historical pageant in the castle grounds in 1908. The players who had prominent speaking parts are watching at the front of the picture.

The pageant consisted of re-enactments of a series of historical scenes from Dudley's past. This scene recalls the events of 1066, the year of the Norman Conquest. Children made up the crowd. on stage

The VIP section of the audience sits waiting for the entertainment to begin at the 1908 Dudley Castle historical pageant. Third from the left at the front is Gilbert Claughton JP, and seventh from the left is Lord Cobham. F.W. Cook is ninth from left, wearing his mayoral chain of office, and to the right of the mayor are the Earl of Dudley and the lady mayoress.

The hydrogen balloon at the 1912 fete is seen close up, with the castle keep in the background. The men are wearing summer boaters and the women are dressed in their best outfits. The balloon was operated by Spencer Brothers of London. Regular ascents were a very popular public attraction in the days before aeroplanes. Nowadays hydrogen would not be allowed as the lifting gas, as it is so flammable. The later airship disasters of the 1930s proved the point.

The castle grounds have long served as a public open space. Here the annual castle fete is being held in the courtyard in around 1912. Crowds of people are watching a large hydrogen balloon being inflated on the left. There is a temporary grandstand on the far left, and a fairground roundabout can be seen.

The entrance to the castle opposite the Great Gate is seen here in 1907. The entrance was next to the servants' block, larder, pantry and kitchen, and therefore was clearly the service access, out of sight of the gentry. This postcard was posted from Truro at 6.30 p.m. on 23 December, to warn the recipient that the sender would arrive on Boxing Day. The card would take longer to arrive these days, of course.

Castle Hill became a densely wooded park. The network of winding paths through the trees was nicknamed Lovers' Walk, which doubtless was one of its main uses. These magnificent slopes of mature trees are now occupied by the zoo buildings, which have not spoiled the beauty of the grounds.

Another part of the castle grounds was also called Lovers' Walk. This card was sent to Miss N. Wright by 'Harry' in 1906, with the message 'Shall be at Top Church at 7 Wednesday evening.' Was the picture of Lovers' Walk some kind of coded message?

Posted in 1915 this card shows the Great Gate, otherwise known as the Triple Gateway. It was built on the north side of the bailey (the castle enclosure). It is defended by two small towers and dates from the twelfth century, with additions from the fourteenth century. There were two portcullises and a drawbridge at the front. It would have been a formidable obstacle to any forces trying to capture the castle.

It is hard to see why the printer has superimposed donkeys on the landscape. Were they a feature of the grounds? An aunt sent this postcard to her nephew in 1911 to show him where she was spending the day.

The Earl of Dudley takes pride of place on this card, which was posted in 1916. He was born William Humble Ward in 1867, succeeding to the title on the death of his father in 1885. The family home was at Himley Hall, a few miles away, until 1937.

The Earl of Dudley's statue is dwarfed by an ornate lamp standard, which is taller than he is. The posters on the gate pillars advertise the fete in around 1912. An enlargement of the left-hand poster reveals that the attractions included the Irish Guards, the Dudley Town Prize Band, balloon ascents, pierrots (pantomime clowns) from Brighton and Hurley & Late, probably a comic turn.

The formal entrance to Dudley Castle and the way in to the annual castle fetes was at the top of Castle Hill. The statue of the first Earl of Dudley had been put there in 1888, paid for by public subscription. This picture was taken in around 1900.

The photographer is looking down Castle Street from Market Place to Castle Hill in the mid-1950s, before the mass redevelopment of this part of the town. The low traffic levels of that era allowed the road sweeper to stand by the traffic island sweeping the gutters in perfect safety.

The Castle Street approach to the castle grounds was lavishly decorated in November 1891. The usual entrance to the castle can be seen through the archway. Also in the archway is a man standing halfway up a ladder, who has managed to attract a small crowd.

Castle Street looking towards Market Place in the mid-1950s. The street looks run-down and shabby. All the shops on the right were soon to be demolished to make way for redevelopments. Frames Tours Ltd were travel agents and sold railway tickets to any destination, a service which is still sadly missed.

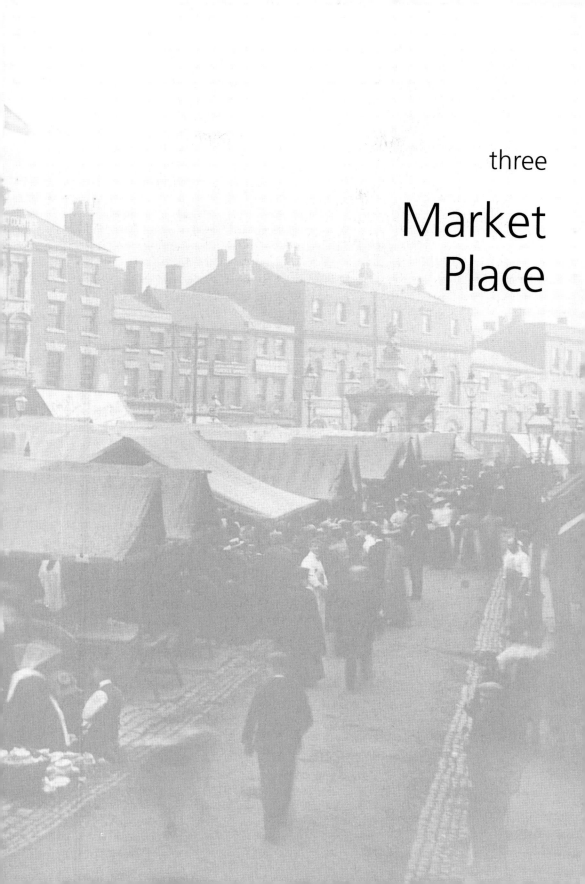

three

Market
Place

The Worcestershire Furnishing Company in Wolverhampton Street had particularly sumptuous showrooms in 1902, when the town was decorated to celebrate the declaration of peace at the end of the Second Boer War. The ornate roofline and glass frontage to the upper floors made this the best-looking shop in the street.

An artist's impression of the Seven Stars pub near the corner of Hall Street, showing that it was originally a seventeenth-century timber-framed building. This must have been a typical design for the town centre buildings before the great rebuilding of Dudley in the eighteenth and nineteenth centuries. The pub was refaced in a mock-Tudor style, but eventually succumbed to redevelopment in the 1960s.

Looking down Market Place over the market stalls (seen here in around 1899) gives an idea of how compact the market area was. The people shopping are quite oblivious to the fact that they are being photographed.

This atmospheric picture dates from 1832, in the days before photography. Subsequent photographs of some of these buildings show that the artist achieved some accuracy. Note the large umbrella-shaped sign above a shop on the left.

In around 1900, S. Sheward's Midland Meat Stores occupied the site now covered by the modern Market Tavern. This is the Castle Street end of Market Place. All of the buildings as far as St Edmund's church have now gone.

This picture must have been taken in the 1850s, because the old town hall was demolished in 1860. The ornate fountain is now on this site. There had been shops behind the town hall in a street called Middle Row, but they were demolished in the 1840s. Encroachment by buildings into the market area was common in the Middle Ages. Posters on the town hall advertise the Dudley Fetes.

STEEDMAN'S
SOOTHING POWDERS
FOR
CHILDREN CUTTING TEETH.

Prepared by

JOHN STEEDMAN, Chemist, Walworth, Surrey.

SPECIAL CAUTION.

The value of this well-known and universally used Family Medicine has been tested in all parts of the world, and by all grades of society for upwards of fifty years. Its large and constantly increasing sale has induced **SPURIOUS IMITATIONS**, in some of which the **Outside Label** and the **Coloured Paper** enclosing the Packet, so closely resemble the **Original** as to have deceived many Purchasers.

Numerous complaints of this kind having been received, the Proprietor feels it due to the thousands of Families in which **Steedman's Soothing Powders** are daily used, to **Caution Purchasers** against these Imitations, and requests their careful attention to the **four following distinctive marks** of the Genuine Medicine.

1st.—That the words " **JOHN STEEDMAN**, Chemist, **Walworth, Surrey**," are **engraved** on the **Government Stamp** affixed to each Packet.

2nd.—Each **Single Powder** has the directions for the dose, and the words " **JOHN STEEDMAN**, Chemist, **Walworth, Surrey**," printed thereon.

3rd.—The name " **STEEDMAN** " is always spelt with two EE's *(and in purchasing, please pronounce the word Steedman as it is printed.)*

4th.—The Manufacture is and always has been carried on " **Solely at Walworth, Surrey**."

Sold by Chemists and Patent Medicine Vendors, in Packets 1s. 1½d., and 2s. 9d.

Sold by C. F. G. CLARK & SON, Chemists,
DUDLEY.

Above: The Dudley and District Benefit Building Society shares the building on the left with T. W. Tanfield's printing office. Next door is H. Cohen's, and the owner might well be the figure standing in the doorway looking at the photographer. This is a row of fine buildings, seen here in 1904, which added to the character of the town.

Left: This advertisement dates from 1881. Even then parents were advised to be very careful what medicines their children were given to take. There is no indication however of what the 'soothing powders' might contain, and these were the days when babies were given laudanum to keep them quiet.

Market Place looked like this around 1900, before the tram lines and overhead cables disfigured it somewhat. A small black and white half-timbered building is on the right edge of the picture. Most of these attractive buildings have now been demolished.

On this card, posted in 1911, is Market Place without its market stalls. It is a quiet sunny afternoon. The pub in the centre on the corner is the Hen and Chickens Inn. The castle looks down on the town, as it has done for over 900 years.

ESTABLISHED OVER 125 YEARS.

General Printing & Stationery

ESTABLISHMENT,

MARKET PLACE (near the Fountain), DUDLEY.

DOYLAH TANFIELD,

(LATE MAURICE.)

Posting Bills, Pamphlets,

CIRCULARS, CARDS, INVOICES,

Programmes, Catalogues, Balance Sheets, Price Lists, Cheque Books, and every description of work, on the shortest notice.

MERCANTILE BOOKS,

And other Manufactured Stationery, in Stock or to Order, with the utmost despatch.

All kinds of PLAIN and ORNAMENTAL BOOKBINDING, in the most Finished Style, and at Moderate Prices.

BEST DRAUGHT & BOTTLED INKS

Always on Sale. Morrell's, Stephens', Lyons, Field's Non-Corrosive, Walkden's, Thacker's, and other well-known makes.

CHOICE SELECTION OF BIBLES, CHURCH SERVICES, PRAYER AND HYMN BOOKS.

Crests, Monograms, Dies, Visiting & Menu Cards, in any style.

Mourning Cards of the Newest Designs

Printed or Engraved to Pattern with despatch.

BOOKS & PERIODICALS IN STOCK & TO ORDER.

Liberal Discount to Schools.

This 1881 advertisement for the General Printing and Stationery shop in Market Place was intended to show off the range of printing fonts available to customers. The inks were available as best draught or bottled from a range of producers, rather like beer.

This early card was posted in 1903. Tramlines run up and down Market Place past the fountain. The overhead power lines are supported by tall posts. Horse transport was still the common form of traffic at this time, and would be for a few more years.

The beautiful lamp-posts round the fountain were gone by 1900, which means that this photograph was taken a little before that. The fountain was built in 1867 to the design of James Forsyth and in a Renaissance style, on the site of the old town hall. It was the gift of the first Earl of Dudley. James Forsyth also designed the Perseus fountain at Witley Court, the country seat of the Earls of Dudley until 1920.

The fountain has not yet been erected in this view from around 1861. This is one of the oldest photographs of Dudley. There is one stall on the empty market patch. It looks like winter, as the shadows are long and everyone has a warm coat on.

This picture was taken from the upper floor of a building in Market Place. The pub in the centre is the Hen and Chickens, and the date is around 1899.

Overleaf: This is the best side of Market Place, seen here in the late 1890s or early 1900s, photographed in what was arguably its heyday. The sequence of premises from Woodhouse along to the Railway Vaults shows evidence of a thriving, bustling town. The buildings range from plain late Georgian in the middle of the picture to ornate mid-Victorian, left of centre. This picture shows the fascinating townscape that can emerge from a random row of differently designed buildings. The tram on the left is being hauled by a steam car.

Market Place and Fountain, Dudley.

A great crowd has gathered in Market Place to listen to the speakers in the middle, who seem to be clergymen. All of the bare-headed young men on the right are standing in rows with heads bowed. It looks like a religious gathering, and there are no banners, so perhaps it is to celebrate soldiers going to or returning from the First World War.

Opposite above: It is a market day in about 1905. A horse and cart wait by the horse trough in the fountain as a tram goes by. The varied range of buildings in the background shows the architectural interest that Dudley has lost over the years.

Opposite below: It can be guessed that this photograph was taken just before the outbreak of the Second World War, judging by the vehicles parked in the street beside the market traders' carts. The flags are flying in the breeze over Peacocks Stores. Maybe it was for Empire Day, or the Silver Jubilee of 1935.

ESTABLISHED 1721.

C. F. G. CLARK & SON,

WHOLESALE AND RETAIL

CHEMISTS AND DRUGGISTS,

238, MARKET PLACE, DUDLEY,

Beg to thank their friends and the public for their liberal patronage and support during the last 40 years, and assure them that their continual efforts will be to secure their continued patronage and consideration.

DRUGS AND CHEMICALS

OF THE GREATEST PURITY AND STRENGTH ALWAYS ON HAND.

PHYSICIANS' PRESCRIPTIONS

And Family Recipes carefully prepared with genuine Drugs & Chemicals.

STEAM PREPARED

PRESERVES & JAMS

OF THE FINEST FRUIT AND FLAVOUR, VIZ. :—

Black Currant Jam, Red Currant, Raspberry, Damson, French Plum, Gooseberry, and Mixed Fruits and Marmalades.

WHOLESALE BOILERS OF ALL KINDS OF

Confectionery Goods and Lozenges.

PICKLE AND SAUCE MAKERS

OF SUPERIOR STRENGTH AND QUALITY.

Wholesale Vinegar Merchants.

ALSO A LARGE ASSORTMENT OF

PATENT MEDICINES AND PERFUMERY

ALWAYS ON HAND.

Above: C.F.G. Clark & Son, of Market Place, offered a wide range of products in this 1881 advertisement. Not surprisingly for the time they felt it important to say that their prescriptions were made up with genuine drugs and chemicals.

Opposite: Mr A. Preedy's Cigar and Tobacco Warehouse at 36 Market Place, seen here in 1908, was the forerunner of a successful chain of tobacconists. The old gentleman on the left puffs on his pipe in silent enjoyment of the shop's product.

SARACEN'S HEAD HOTEL. STONE STREET. DUDLEY.

DINING AND GRILL ROOM
BILLIARDS

GARAGE

PROPRIETOR—C. E. KING.   Tel. 2326

The Saracen's Head Hotel has dominated the view of this street since the 1840s, when the present building was erected. It was a centre for Freemasons and Nonconformists. It was owned by the Hanson family, who eventually ran Julia Hanson's brewery, brewing fine mild ale. The brewery was later taken over by Banks's.

The Dudley Exhibition in 1887 was celebrated by decorating Market Place. The banner on Walmsley's shop welcoming the Countess of Dudley means that she was probably opening or visiting the exhibition. The family had long since moved out of Dudley itself.

George Mason's grocers shop at 38 Market Place, in around 1912. These were the days of well-staffed shops. There are fifteen people visible in the picture. The display of hams hanging outside the shop would not be allowed today. Notice the two ornate lamps hanging in front of the windows. The shop closed in 1969.

Richardson's clothes shop was in Market Place. Presumably it catered for the cheaper end of the men's jacket and trouser trade. This photograph was taken in 1926. One of the Richardson family is posing on the left outside the shop in his best suit. The word 'Peoples' shows that signwriters have always had problems with apostrophes.

Opposite: The statue of local footballing hero Duncan Edwards in Market Place was erected in 1999 to commemorate his life. Born in Dudley in 1936 he made 175 appearances for Manchester United and won eighteen England caps before he was killed in the Munich air disaster in 1958 when the plane carrying Manchester United players, backroom staff and journalists crashed in a blizzard on take-off. Twenty-three passengers died.

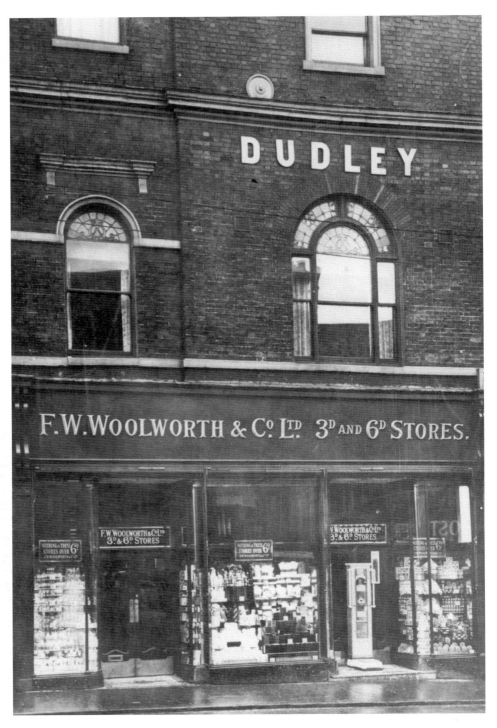

F.W. Woolworth began trading in Britain in 1909 when the American parent company started a worldwide expansion. The first store was in Liverpool, and then the chain rapidly expanded across the country. The shop front – seen here sometime before 1930 – is quite restrained, and does not seem out of place on the late eighteenth-century building.

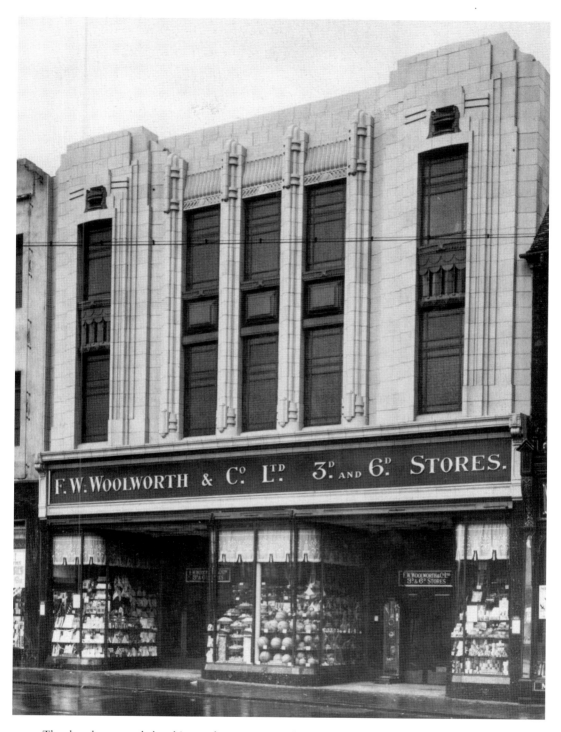

The shop has expanded and is seen here on a rainy day in the 1930s. This is a good example of the modern style of the decade, and the upper floors remain recognisably the same today. A weighing machine stands in the shop doorway. The shop boasted that you didn't need to ask the price, everything was either 3d or 6d.

By the early 1960s there were only two old buildings left on this side of Market Place; Boots the Chemist, and then another a little further down. All the rest had been replaced by modern buildings or refronted in a modern style, no doubt providing much better amenities for customers, but much of the former atmosphere has been lost.

Opposite above: In the 1930s this was the view down Market Place over the stalls to the castle. The scene had changed little from Victorian times.

Opposite below: These shoppers are thronging around the open stalls in Market Place some time in the 1970s. Like most open markets the stalls were only allowed to trade on certain days of the week.

Seen here during the 1980s, Woolworths has modernised its ground floor entrance. The 1930s detailing on the upper floors has considerably more character than the plain, characterless block of Littlewoods next door.

four

The Shops

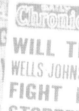

John Hollins' bold and simple name board over his jewellery shop in Wolverhampton Street, *c.* 1890. This style of building is typically Victorian, and is still to be seen in some small towns in Ireland. Note the lamps angled over the windows to light up the stock, and the giant display watch in the case by the door.

J. Anyon's lamp shop in Wolverhampton Street. This photograph was taken just before the First World War. The shop sold lamp oil as well as lamps. The oil lamp trade declined in the 1920s, and the shop diversified into the new craze – wireless parts.

A greengrocers in Stone Street with open frontage, around 1910. To this day many small greengrocers' shops are unheated in order to keep the produce as fresh as possible. The patient horse has probably brought the baskets of produce from the market to be unloaded at the shop.

We can see down High Street to Market Place, with the castle on the far horizon, in this view dating from the very early 1900s. A horse and cart plods up the empty street past a splendid array of Georgian and Victorian shop fronts, followed by a tram. The YMCA is on the left in the Temperance Institute building.

W.L. Dudley & Co. on Castle Street between 1900 and 1910. The shop sells boot polish, rubber heels and something called a revolving heel. Presumably it could be turned round to even out wear. In the window is a poster for 'electric pictures' at the public hall, which was in Wolverhampton Street.

This photograph from 1957 shows assorted shops on the corner of Stone Street and High Street, located in a stylish early nineteenth-century Regency building. They are starting to look a little run-down.

The same building in 2004; it now has a branch of Thomas Cook, the travel agents, on the corner. It has been sympathetically restored, but the block would benefit from using a uniform colouring scheme on the upper floors and the replacement of the missing sash windows.

F.W. Cook's curtain and carpet shop, pictured in the 1890s. The building style dates from the second half of the nineteenth century, when more and more decoration was being added to front elevations. It is not clear why there are two bicycles hanging up in the window over the carpet rolls, but the 1890s were the heyday of the cycling craze and perhaps Cook's were cashing in on the boom.

This picture of High Street from 1957 is very interesting on close inspection. On the left is an early nineteenth-century building which has been turned into three shops. The pram shop has converted an upstairs window into a larger plate glass one. Victoria House (on the right) has a bold original Victorian nameplate on the upper storeys.

Spiers, the furniture shop, was in High Street and had a simple Victorian frontage with cut brick arches over the windows. The ground floor frontage, photographed in 1957, is a modern but tasteful alteration that does not spoil the look of the building.

The Bytheway's newsagent and tobacconist on Wolverhampton Street. It may have sold books too, judging by the right-hand window. The news of uprisings, strikes, royal revelations and the Worcester Music Festival could be from almost any year, but the Bombardier Billy Wells *v.* Jack Johnson fight took place in October 1911.

Opposite above: This is a later picture of the Bytheway's shop in Wolverhampton Street, perhaps from the 1930s, but there is little clue in the news placards. A sign of the times is the rack of rent books hanging by the door.

Opposite below: G.J. Taylor was a newsagent and hairdresser on the corner of High Street and Stafford Street. This photograph is from 1926. The very dilapidated Three Crowns next door seems to have been converted from a timber-framed cottage, the evidence for which is on the side gable.

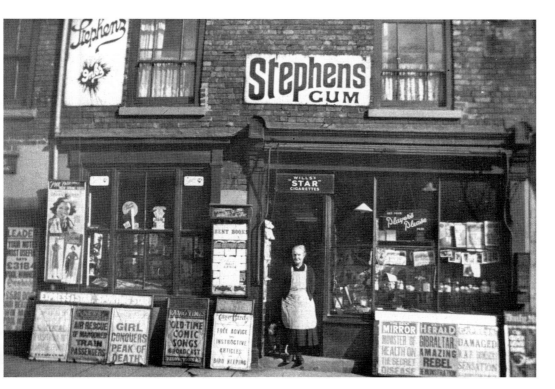

Of the few old buildings of merit still to be seen in Market Square, these two are fortunately side by side. The one on the left is early Victorian and the other one dates from early in the twentieth century. They would both benefit from a more sympathetic treatment at ground floor level, especially the Fountain Arcade frontage.

It is a quiet morning in the 1920s in this photograph, looking up High Street to St Thomas' church. The rather humble buildings past the bank on the left face their more ornate Victorian counterparts. Their unbroken sequence nevertheless makes a satisfying addition to the street scene.

The upper end of High Street as it rises towards St Thomas' church (*c*. 1900) shows a contrast in prosperity. On the left the buildings are mass-built Victorian houses which have been turned into little shops. On the right the shops are better built, more stylish and look more prosperous. Note the heavy railings and gate on the right giving privacy to one large house.

Decorated in 1902 to celebrate the Coronation of King Edward VII, High Street has flags and bunting everywhere. The paperboys in the middle of the road are probably selling the Coronation Day special edition of a local or national newspaper.

High Street connected Market Place and St Thomas' church, just discernible here in this view from around 1908. The beautifully ornate posts hold the overhead tram wires. This was one of the main shopping streets in the town. Just above the lady on the left, a giant pair of spectacles advertises an optician; opposite is the ornate shop front of Edward Grey, fancy drapers.

Wolverhampton Street was at its most impressive between 1900 and 1910. It is still the most interesting street architecturally in Dudley, despite the loss of many fine buildings to redevelopment.

Above: This is the imposing facade of Bunce's, the draper in High Street. It is a lovely example of modernistic art deco styling. This photograph dates from the 1930s, when the fascia had just been redesigned.

Above: Melias Ltd in Hall Street in 1958. The double-fronted ground floor fascia conceals the fact that the shop apparently occupies two adjoining buildings knocked into one. The upper windows on the right are from the late eighteenth century.

Opposite below: This is Bunce's in 1957. The upper floors have ornate Victorian gothic windows and mouldings. The frontage however is awkwardly divided on the ground floor between Bunce's and Bunney's, a glass and china shop.

Gray's of Dudley, the famous sweet shop, is very much an institution in the town. This is Teddy Gray, the son of John Gray, standing in the doorway of the Wolverhampton Street shop sometime in the 1920s or 1930s, judging by the style of the suit. Gray's make their own sweets, and their herbal tablets are a local speciality.

This is Teddy Gray Senior (of the sweet-manufacturing family) at the reins of the shop delivery cart. There are two horses in harness for some reason, the front one held by a groom. The cart could not have been so heavy that it needed two horses to pull it. Perhaps this postcard was just to indicate that Mr Gray had two horses and was a man of standing in the town.

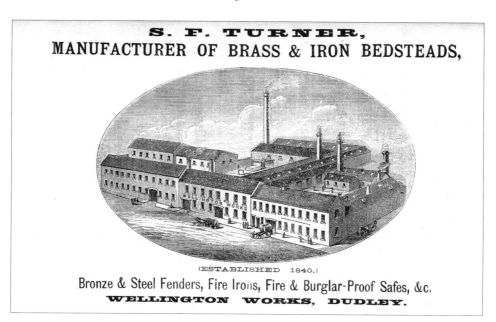

This advertisement showing a manufacturer's premises dates from 1881. It was typical of medium-sized factories in the Black Country.

In 1876 the manager of Old Bank in Wolverhampton Street arrives by carriage and poses outside for the photographer with a female companion, perhaps his wife. The manager's name was George Wilkinson. The bank was an example of elegant eighteenth-century architecture which has now sadly been lost.

The Empire Theatre in Hall Street is seen here being demolished in the 1970s. This variety theatre was built in 1903 and was turned into a cinema in 1912. It closed in 1940.

This building, home to the art gallery, art school and library, was built in 1887. It was built with attractive red bricks, but had lost its original corner turret by the time this modern photograph was taken. Building costs were met from the proceeds of the Earl of Dudley's annual Whitsun fete.

This was the original police station, built in the 1840s with a castellated gatehouse and tower. The new police station in New Street replaced it, but the building survived to become council offices, which are still there today.

THE GRAND MEDICINE OF THE DAY!

SQUIRE KNIGHT'S

CELEBRATED

PURIFYING FAMILY PILLS.

These celebrated Pills have for the last HUNDRED YEARS proved very superior to every other Medicine offered to the Public in the cure of Indigestion, Bilious Complaints, Loss of Appetite, Sick Headache, Giddiness in the Head, Pain and Fulness after Meals, Wind, Heartburn, Lowness of Spirits, Piles, Worms, Shortness of Breath, Nervous Disease, Cramps, Spasms, Fevers, Affections of the Liver, Dimness of Sight, Pains in the Stomach and Bowels, Eruptions of the Skin, &c., &c.

TESTIMONIALS.

Mrs. Job Stephens, of Woodside, Dudley, was perfectly cured of Wind and Spasms, of one year's duration, by taking these celebrated Pills.

Amelia Griffiths, of Mostyn, was cured of nine years' affliction of Indigestion by taking two boxes of these Pills.

Joseph Wagstaff, of Dudley Port, was afflicted with a severe Pain in his Side for four years, but was cured before he had taken two boxes of these Pills.

Mrs. Davis, of Kingswinford, was cured of constant Costiveness, Pains in the Bowels, and Giddiness in the Head, by taking these Pills.

Susannah Brewster, Herbert Street, Wolverhampton, was cured of a very bad Liver Complaint by taking "Squire Knight's Purifying Pills."

Henry McKay, Woodside, Dudley, has proved these Pills to be the best for Indigestion, Wind, Heartburn, and a Disordered Stomach.

Mrs. Beard, High Street, Bradley, was cured of a very serious Outbreak, arising from Impurities in the Blood, besides relieving a Congested Liver, and acting upon the Stomach and Bowels.

PREPARED BY

C. F. G. CLARK & SON,

(SUCCESSORS TO SQUIRE KNIGHT),

CHEMISTS, MARKET PLACE, DUDLEY.

Sold by Messrs. Morgan and Lawley, Hewitt, Homes Grove, and Roberts, Kidderminster; Mellor, Malvern; Cooper, Upton; Haines, Bromsgrove; Hughes, Morris, Hemming, and Levi, Stourbridge; Jones, Lye Waste; Bishop and Matthews, Cradley Heath; Darby and Sidaway, Cradley; Cox, Old Hill; Briggs and Nicklin, Tipton; Rooker, Ford and Addison, Brierley Hill; Pearson, Kingswinford; Hudson, Green, Williams, and Burch, West Bromwich; Frampton and Dancer, Smethwick; Price, Spon Lane; Hipkiss, Princes End; Torbitt and Gittings, Oldbury; Butler, Darlaston; Skirving, Emery, and Morris, Wednesbury; Rudge, Bradley, Hyde, Coseley; and Collins, Brettell Lane.

Sold in Boxes, 7½d., 1s.1½d., 2s.9d., and 4s.6d. each.

An 1881 advertisement for Clarks the Chemist features an impressive set of testimonials from satisfied local consumers. For the equivalent of three pence a box, a wide range of common ailments could be cured with Squire Knight's 'Purifying Family Pills', although in two cases more than one box was clearly required.

Opposite above: G.H. Wright's shop, seen here in the 1930s, was on the corner of Hall Street. Wright's provided a complete home furnishing service. In the right-hand window at the back of the shop there is some kitchen furniture that would have been seen in most households before the war. The front flap folded down to make a work surface, usually enamel, and food was kept in cupboards above and below it.

Opposite below: As part of their service in the 1930s G.H. Wright's also delivered furniture, and would use one of their vans to move your belongings when you moved house. It is a sign of the times that removal vans are a lot bigger these days.

The Top Rank club in High Street started life in the 1920s as the Regent cinema. It was relaunched as the Gaumont cinema after the war, and then as the Top Rank bingo club in 1961.

Fosters clothing shop in Market Place in the mid-1980s. This style of shop front can still be seen today. The shop name occupies a minor position beneath the long, empty area over the windows. The mirror-finish panels at the side reflect the rain-covered bricks of the pedestrian zone.

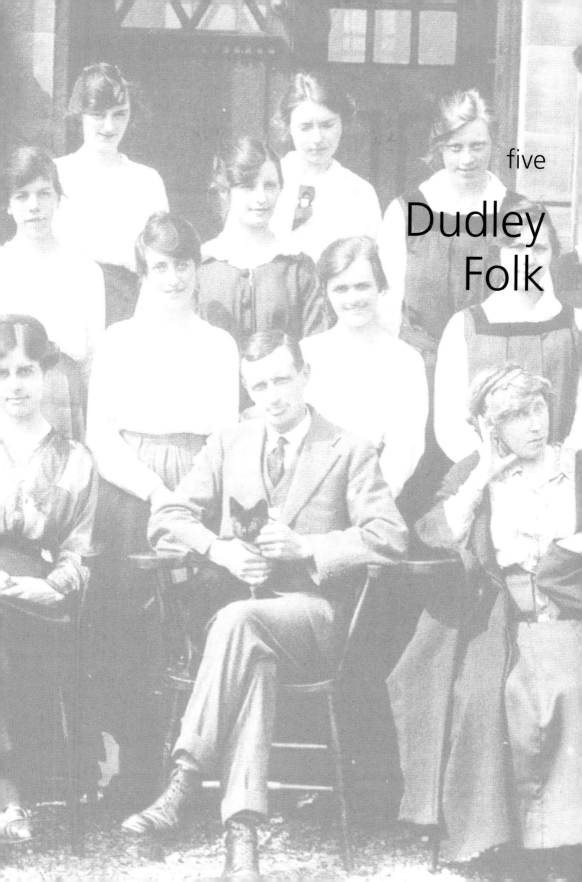

five

Dudley
Folk

Left: Edward Brookes, photographed here around 1860, was a butcher in High Street. He was born in Alveley, Staffordshire in 1807, but settled and spent his life in Dudley.

Below: Edward Brookes died in 1879 and was buried in St Thomas' churchyard. His son, also named Edward Brookes, grew up in Dudley and went on to run his own butchers shop in Kingswinford.

"SIMPLY TO THY CROSS I CLING."

In Loving Memory of

Edward Brookes,

Late of High Street, Dudley, Who Died 16th June, 1879, Aged 72 Years.

———

Interred in St. Thomas's Burial Ground, on the 20th June.

Left: Ben Boucher, the Dudley poet, in 1847. He composed what are in truth not very good poems on any public event that took his fancy. He had them printed on broadsheets and sold them at a penny each. He died in 1851 in a workhouse.

On the demolition of old St Thomas' church he wrote:

The seats and the windows, ah, and the clock too,
Were sent on to Gornal, to their Gornal crew;
For the sand men and asses, for to go to church,
And the people of Dudley were left in the lurch.

Below: Dudley Congregational church football club in about 1910. Many churches organised football teams that played in local leagues. The equivalent today would be the large number of amateur teams from local pubs that play in Sunday leagues.

The Dudley-born Wright brothers were famous aviation pioneers. Their father owned a factory that made chains and boilers. This is Howard Wright, who helped design the boiler for Hiram Maxim's steam-powered aircraft in the nineteenth century. With his brother Warwick he founded an aircraft company in 1907 in Hammersmith.

The Wright brothers claimed to be the first true aircraft manufacturers in Britain. Thomas Sopwith learned to fly in one of their biplanes. Warwick Wright, shown here in the 1920s, later became Chief Designer for the Samuel White Company on the Isle of Wight.

Above: Hop pickers, seen here on their way to the hop fields in carts, probably in the 1890s. Hop picking was a traditional annual event for many families until comparatively recently. Although it could be hard work, it was probably the equivalent of a holiday in the country for many Black Country folk.

Left: These hop pickers are posing in the fields by the hops in the 1900s. They lived on the farm during the picking season and were usually given barns to sleep in that had been cleaned, divided up into family units and equipped with blankets and straw.

After picking, the piles of hops were measured so as to work out how much each family had picked – they were paid by the bushel – before the hops were taken from the fields in horse-drawn carts. The slump in hop prices in the 1930s and the 1944 Education Act meant that mechanised picking gradually replaced manual labour, so that by the 1970s most farms no longer took on manual pickers.

The hop farms and hop yards were numerous and families often went to work at the same one every year, where they would be treated as old friends. Most of the families doing the picking came down from the Black Country, the nearest source of a large, cheap labour force.

In the early 1900s, Dudley hop pickers went by train to get to the hop farms in Herefordshire or Worcestershire. The trains went down the Hereford railway line, and many of the farms were situated on either side of the line

These children, queuing outside the Odeon at Castle Hill, were taking part in a salvage collection competition in the 1940s. Goods were in short supply in Britain in the immediate post-war period, and everything was recycled or repaired as far as possible. 'Make do and mend' was the order of the day.

Opposite above: This picture is dated 1924. The students at Dudley Teacher Training College are dressed in home-made costumes for the May Festival. They manage to look remarkably gloomy, maybe because they were faced with a career in schools when they qualified.

Opposite below: The female day students at Dudley Teacher Training College pose for a group picture outside the college building sometime between 1910 and 1920. The tutor in the middle of the front row is stroking a black cat. Could it be the college cat?

A large group of female trainee teachers at Dudley Teacher Training College pose for the photographer sometime in the 1950s. What was the significance of the striped jackets? Did the college have a uniform?

This is a group of trainee teachers at the college, probably in the 1950s, who would have gone on to teach in the 1960s. Although they were mostly young men, they are dressed in a style which makes them look older than they were. In the 1950s there was no such thing as teenage clothing – teenage boys used to dress like their fathers.

A group of female trainee teachers pose demurely outside the college on a sunny day. The college merged with Wolverhampton Polytechnic in the late 1970s, when teacher training was reorganised and several local colleges lost their autonomy.

The Miners' Arms cribbage club, winners of the Dudley East Cribbage League Cup in 1953 and 1954. From left to right, back row: I. Fisher, E. Turner, L. Boylen, L. Alexander. Front row: S. Morcom, H. Johnson, J. Darby, S. Dukes, A. Rushton, G. Yale, A. Alexander.

A Christmas party for children in 1954 at the West End Hotel on Wolverhampton Street. The licensees, Mr and Mrs Whitehouse, were the hosts and seventy guests attended.

Eighty senior citizens in 1960, on their annual outing from the Selbourne pub in Dudley to Bourton-on-the-Water in the Cotswolds. Afterwards they had a chicken dinner at Wychbold.

six

Entertainments

We are looking up Castle Hill in around 1900. The horse trough in front of the Station Hotel was originally at the top of the hill. It dated from 1862 and was replaced outside the entrance to the castle by the Earl of Dudley's statue. It was removed completely just as it reached its centenary.

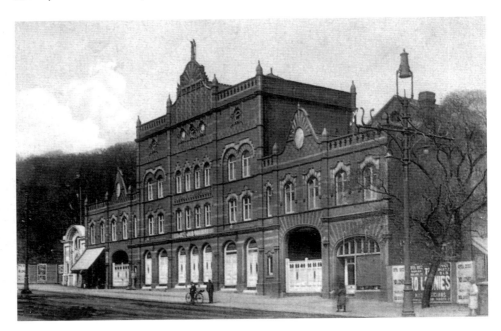

The opera house was a grand building, opened in 1899 and seen here very shortly afterwards. It was run by local theatre entrepreneur John Maurice Clement. During its first week the renowned D'Oyly Carte company put on a selection of Gilbert and Sullivan's great comic operas. Always a successful venture, the theatre was destroyed by fire in 1936. It was replaced by the Dudley Hippodrome in 1938.

Amy Hill, from the Hippodrome ticket office, is sitting outside the theatre in around 1944. The show *Soldiers in Skirts*, although sponsored by the American military, was banned by the Dudley Watch Committee on its first tour, as it may have given the wrong image of the soldiery in wartime.

The Hippodrome celebrated its eighth birthday in fine style with a giant onstage birthday cake. The gentleman in the grey suit holding the hat is Jimmy James, a superb old-time comedian with impeccable timing.

In the Hippodrome pantomime in 1947, Billy Russell played Billy Crusoe. Billy Russell was a rare thing, a Black Country comedian who was a national success, and who made several comedy records in the 1930s. His stock character was a scruffy working-class man. Another celebrated comic, Tony Hancock, also appeared here in 1947, and then again in 1951 in the *Educating Archie* stage show.

Lona Jones plays the lead in *Robinson Crusoe* at the Hippodrome in the 1947 pantomime. The Latour Babes (seen taking a bow in front of the chorus) recently held a reunion, more than fifty years later.

DUDLEY HIPPODROME

England's most modern variety theatre

Left: A Hippodrome programme from May 1960. 'England's most modern variety theatre' was reduced to staging an entertainment entitled *Strike a Nude Note*. It is a matter of debate whether this kind of show killed off variety theatres, or whether they were in terminal decline already by the 1960s.

Below: Jack White, the impeccably dressed Hippodrome front of house manager, addresses the audience from centre stage after another pantomime performance, probably in the late 1940s.

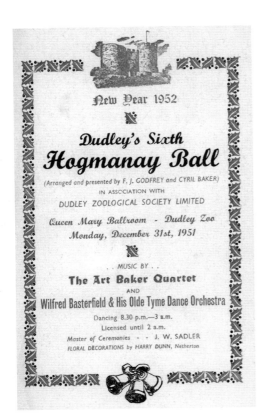

New Year 1952

Dudley's Sixth
Hogmanay Ball

(Arranged and presented by F. J. GODFREY and CYRIL BAKER)
IN ASSOCIATION WITH
DUDLEY ZOOLOGICAL SOCIETY LIMITED

Queen Mary Ballroom - Dudley Zoo
Monday, December 31st, 1951

. . MUSIC BY . .
The Art Baker Quartet
AND
Wilfred Basterfield & His Olde Tyme Dance Orchestra

Dancing 8.30 p.m.—3 a.m.
Licensed until 2 a.m.
Master of Ceremonies - - J. W. SADLER
FLORAL DECORATIONS by HARRY DUNN, Netherton

Left: There are currently plans to redevelop the zoo site after years of poor maintenance and investment. The emphasis is on regenerating the zoo and castle as tourist attractions and widening the use of the facilities. This is not a new idea though, as evidenced by this ball programme from 1951. The Queen Mary Ballroom is an excellent example of the buildings designed by the Tecton firm in the 1930s.

Below: The Plaza began as the Colosseum on Castle Hill in 1910. It was renamed the John Bull, then the Scala and finally became the Plaza in 1931. The Hippodrome replaced the opera house when it burned down in 1936. This view is from 1981.

The entrance to the zoo was on Castle Hill. The zoo opened in the castle grounds in 1937. The Dudley Zoological Society had been founded in 1935; its aim was to develop the castle site into an economical venture.

From the heights of the castle there was a fine view down to the entrance. Thousands of visitors queued to gain entry in the first winter of opening. The zoo buildings are scattered around the castle grounds.

Above: The elephant house was one of thirteen original pavilions. They were all designed by Tecton and Berthold Lubetkin. All the buildings made full use of the sculptural potential of concrete and the challenging woodland slopes.

Left: The polar bear pit is a fine example of a building meant to be as significant and interesting to look at as the animals inside. The open nature of the buildings and the excellent views they gave visitors were completely new in the 1930s.

Opposite above: This early leaflet for the Black Country Museum (dating from 1974) was given out in libraries. It described how the museum would have an open-air layout to show the development of the Black Country through the ages. The exhibits had been accumulating since 1966 and would be augmented by reconstructed buildings, creating a replica Black Country hamlet.

Opposite below: A view of rescued buildings during reconstruction. Great care is taken to preserve the look and feel of each building. The current intention is to double the size of the museum in a £10 million development plan between 2005 and 2015.

The Black Country Museum

This building, dating from the mid-nineteenth century, was moved to the museum from Wolverhampton in 1980. It has been fitted out as a hardware shop. It has obviously been altered to some extent, as the building had a large shop front on the left and a small window on the right before it was taken down.

Here is the building as it was in the 1970s in Pipers Row, Wolverhampton. It was occupied by a newsagent and had become very run down, as the area around it had been blighted by the prospect of demolition.

The 1879 cast-iron bridge was designed by C. Eastlake Thom of Wolverhampton. It was in the way of the new ring road and was dismantled by West Midlands County Council contractors in 1976. It was given to the Black Country Museum despite strenuous opposition from some Wolverhampton councillors, who wanted it re-erected in its home town.

The Black Country Museum, now called the Black Country Living Museum, occupies a 26-acre reclaimed industrial site. A tramway connects the Tipton Road entrance with the main hamlet at the other end of the site.

Looking over the bridge past a row of shops and houses on the left of the Bottle and Glass pub. The museum's hamlet is used very frequently for school visits. For the children this is all a reflection of the distant past, but the sweetshop, chip shop and funfair make it a good outing.

seven

Notable
Buildings

Dudley Girls High School, designed by J. Hutchings and built in 1910 in a loose, decorative, late seventeenth-century style. The building is seen here on a nice sunny day in the 1920s; it has sadly now been demolished.

Upper Standard School in Dudley, around 1910. High-rise was the fashion in school buildings in those days. When the Boer War Memorial was unveiled in 1904 this school hosted a ceremonial lunch, after the procession from the town hall via Queen's Cross cemetery, for the Imperial Yeomanry and the Dudley Volunteers.

Dudley Training College was a teacher training centre. It opened in 1910 in what were thought at the time to be flamboyant buildings. This card was posted by a student in October 1916. She says there are two lady inspectors there. The Zeppelins had been out again the previous night, but the students didn't find out until the next day.

The Right Honourable Georgina, Countess of Dudley laying the foundation stone for the new public library in St James' Road in 1908. The countess was the second wife of the first earl and lived from 1846 to 1929.

The free library in St James' Road was built in 1908 and 1909, designed by George H. Wenyon. The style is early English baroque. The library stood alone until the town hall was built next to it in 1928.

The new town hall was built next to the library in St James' Road in 1928. It was awarded a Royal Institute of British Architects medal for the best provincial building. This picture dates from the 1930s.

The old council house in Priory Road, seen here in the 1920s. These buildings had been the home of the council since 1870, which is apparently when they were built. They were replaced in the mid-1930s by the present council buildings.

The post office in Wolverhampton Street was originally a red-brick building built in 1879 and 1880. It was extended several times as business grew and in 1909 this imposing stone façade replaced the brick one. This picture was taken shortly after the post office was built.

Wolverhampton Street is still the best-preserved street in Dudley, with good-quality buildings. The houses are now mainly offices and range from the early eighteenth century (Finch House) to the early twentieth century (the post office) on the right of the picture.

Left: The Weights and Measures building in Stone Street in around 1910. Today the use of this square has gone almost full circle; over the course of a hundred years it has changed from a public market space to a bus terminus, and then back to a public open space.

Below: The demolition here in Stone Street is being carried out in April 1938 by S.V. Whitehouse, of the Round Street Garage in Netherton. The Fountain Arcade was built next to this site in 1925.

The Priory of St James dates from around 1160. Here are the ruins in their most romantic and overgrown state, c. 1910. Most of this foliage has been cut away now, leaving the building looking very bare and lacking in atmosphere. The priory church still stood in the sixteenth century and contained monuments and effigies of the Lords of Dudley.

The priory was founded for Cluniac Benedictines by the Norman baron of Dudley, Gervase Paganel. The remnants of the buildings were used as a thread manufactory in the eighteenth and nineteenth centuries. The picturesque ruins are seen here in around 1900.

In the 1930s the ruins looked much as they had done for centuries. They belonged to the castle until they were sold to Dudley Council in 1926. Nowadays the council tries to keep them in their current state, while preserving them from further decay.

Priory Hall was built in the priory grounds in around 1825, in an early Tudor style, as the main residence of the principal agent of the Dudley Estate. Sir Gilbert Claughton lived there until he died in 1921. The land and priory were bought by Dudley Council in 1926.

Before the estate was redeveloped for residential use and as parkland in the 1920s, the priory grounds were an unspoiled area of beauty, consisting of man-made parkland with a fine view of the castle on its wooded hill (seen here in around 1910).

DUDLEY CASTLE FROM PRIORY GARDENS.

Dating from around 1905, this is a detailed photographic view of a gardener posing with his barrow in the priory gardens, which were part of Priory Hall. All of this area is now occupied by housing and public open space.

St Thomas' church was built between 1815 and 1818, to the design of William C. Brooks. It replaced the medieval church, which was in poor repair and was demolished in 1815 by order of the vicar, Dr Luke Booker, a prominent force in the town. St Thomas' is built of Tixall stone in perpendicular style, but the pale stone seen here in 1918 suffered badly from pollution and became very dark. The churchyard still has an impressive collection of well-carved nineteenth-century memorials, which would have been expensive to buy.

This interior view of St Thomas' church is difficult to date, but the postcard is from the early 1900s. The original groined roof of the nave fell down suddenly in 1892, and it was discovered that it had been constructed from plaster, rather than stone.

St Edmund's church in Castle Street, seen in this postcard of 1903, was built of brick and stone between 1722 and 1724. This church replaced a medieval one demolished during an attack on the castle in 1646.

This beautiful hand-tinted postcard of 1905 shows the east window of St Thomas' church. St Thomas', the parish church of Dudley, was also known as Top Church, and stands at the top of High Street. This window was created in 1821 by J. Blacker. It depicts the Transfiguration, copied from a Raphael original. It is painted (not coloured) glass, and is positioned several feet inside the real window, with a linen sheet behind it to diffuse the light.

The war memorial paying tribute to the soldiers of Dudley who died in the Boer War (1899-1902) was designed by Henry Owen Burgess, of Old Hill. It cost about £300 to make and was paid for by public subscription. It was unveiled on 23 September 1904 by Lt-Gen. Sir Neville Gerald Lyttelton. Out of 300 Dudley soldiers, fifty-six had died in the war.

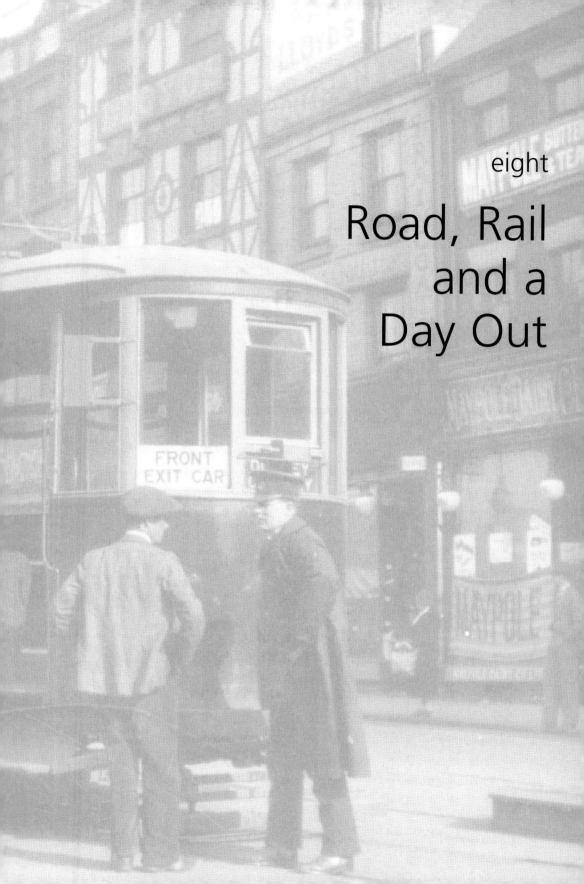

eight

Road, Rail
and a
Day Out

This is a rare photograph of an 1898 tramcar on the Dudley & Stourbridge tramway, waiting outside the Station Hotel just by Dudley railway station. Notice that there are no advertisements on the sides of the tram.

A tram waits by Dudley station, next to the Station Hotel, in the summer of 1936. It advertises Dewars whisky and Typhoo tea (try it 'for indigestion'). This type of tram was completely enclosed on the top deck.

Two electric trams pass each other in front of the fountain in Market Place. Built in 1901, cars 39 to 42 (which each had sixty-four seats) were transferred to Wolverhampton District Electric Tramways in 1904 from the Dudley, Stourbridge & District Electric Traction Company.

A Wolverhampton trolleybus on service No. 58 is just turning into the Stone Street terminus in the early 1960s. The Saracens Head is in the background. The buildings by the bus have in recent years been carefully restored.

This is a tram on the Dudley to Tividale route, seen in 1917 in Market Place. The tram advertises de Kuypers gin. It belonged to the Dudley & Stourbridge Electric Tramway. Trams are now reappearing on the streets of some towns.

Opposite above: Tram No. 30 is making its way down Wolverhampton Street out of town in around 1900. The ride upstairs on the open top was popular on sunny days such as this. The Crown stands guard on the corner of the street.

Opposite below: A Wolverhampton-built Sunbeam trolleybus leaves Dudley for Wolverhampton in the mid-1960s, turning right into Wolverhampton Street round the post office. The bus was painted in the Wolverhampton livery of pale yellow and green.

The last passenger service to Dudley station was in 1964; the station was demolished in 1967. The last employees at the station survey the sad devastation just before demolition.

Opposite above: In 1967 a new freightliner terminal was built on the station site to handle container traffic. This was believed at the time to be the future of road/rail transport. Here the giant crane that loaded and unloaded the freight containers can be seen on its gantry.

Opposite below: The last train left the terminal in 1986 and the line was completely closed in 1992. This is the sad scene after the freightliner terminal had been closed and stripped of everything salvageable.

Dudley's railway station is seen here from Station Drive in around 1900. The station was below road level and good views could be had from the road bridge. The first trains had reached Dudley in 1849, and the service was formally inaugurated in 1850.

A parcels train stands at the platform in 1963, facing north. Within a very few years the steam locomotive on the left would be obsolete as diesel trains took over. Enthusiasts were able to rescue and preserve a few of the steam trains.

Left: In 1963 this was the view south down the station platform from the footbridge to the main road bridge and the Station Hotel.

Below: A line of Palethorpes' sausage vans waits at the station in 1962. The famous local sausage-making company had a private fleet of vans, painted in its own colours, for transporting its products.

The Glynne Arms, up a lane off the Himley Road, was on the estate of the Earl of Dudley. It was a popular destination for walkers, pony traps and cyclists when these pictures were taken in around 1900. The surroundings are still attractive today, although most of the foreground is now a car park.

A remarkable optical illusion could be seen in the tap room, as a marble would apparently roll up a long table. Even the view of the surrounding normal countryside through the window did not spoil the effect.

The popularity and public curiosity in the pub in the 1900s meant that many views were preserved of the typical Victorian pub interior. This is the refreshment room. Note how the grandfather clock, which had to be vertical because of its pendulum, appears to lean alarmingly away from the wall.

The bar room has an advertising placard for Bass Old Strong Ale and a calendar from Julia Hanson, a well-known local brewery. The bottles on the shelves are level; everything else is not. The pub was known to everyone as The Crooked House or The Siden House, as it had been undermined by coal workings and the land had subsided. The house had severely tilted and was supported by buttresses, but was otherwise intact.

Other local titles published by Tempus

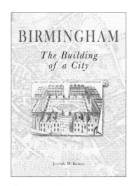

Birmingham The Building of a City
JOSEPH MCKENNA

Since the time of William Hutton's history of Birmingham in 1780, there has been no real attempt to describe and explain the physical growth of Birmingham as a city and to consider why it developed in the way it did. When was the growth and why did it occur? Who were the men who designed, financed and built modern Birmingham? This fascinating book provides answers to these important questions and more.

0 7524 3489 6

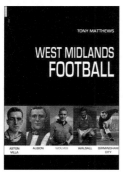

West Midlands Football
TONY MATTHEWS

Focusing on five clubs – Aston Villa, Birmingham City, West Bromwich Albion, Wolverhampton Wanderers and Walsall – this is the story of League and cup football in the West Midlands: the great players, passionately fought local derbies, and the successes and failures that have inspired countless fans over the years. The highs and lows are recounted here in a fine illustrated history that is sure to delight all fans who have followed the game in these parts.

0 7524 3270 2

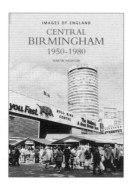

Central Birmingham 1950-1980
MARTIN HAMPSON

This pictorial history traces some of the dramatic developments that have taken place in the centre of Birmingham during three decades. It recalls a bygone age when the Bull Ring's open market sloped down from the High Street to St Martin's, when trams trundled down Victorian streets and steam trains still halted at soot-blackened stations. This collection of over 200 photographs, each accompanied by supporting text, shows how the foundations of present-day Birmingham were laid.

0 7524 3361 X

Walsall Leather Industry
The World's Saddlers
MICHAEL GLASSON

For nearly 200 years Walsall has been a major centre of leather industry, exporting saddles, bridles and a variety of horse equipment to most corners of the world. At its peak the industry employed over 10,000 men and women, with the British Army being the single biggest customer. These days Walsall maintains an international reputation for its products, and not surprisingly the town has been called the saddlery 'capital' of the world.

0 7524 2793 8

⌐ing other books published by Tempus, or in case you have difficulty finding any
    ‿op, you can also place orders directly through our website